50 Canadian Dishes for the House

By: Kelly Johnson

Table of Contents

- Poutine
- Butter Tarts
- Nanaimo Bars
- Tourtière
- Bannock
- Caesar Cocktail
- BeaverTails
- Peameal Bacon Sandwich
- Maple-Glazed Salmon
- Split Pea Soup
- Montreal Smoked Meat Sandwich
- Maple Syrup Pie
- Lobster Roll
- Chicken and Wild Rice Soup
- Saskatoon Berry Pie
- Maple-Glazed Donuts
- Salmon Candy

- Cream of Mushroom Soup
- Blueberry Grunt
- Rappie Pie
- Fish and Brewis
- Indian Butter Chicken
- Ginger Beef
- Ketchup Chips
- Maple-Glazed Carrots
- Wild Game Stew
- Pea Soup with Ham
- Blueberry Buckle
- Maple Baked Beans
- Clam Chowder
- Cabbage Rolls
- Wild Blueberry Pancakes
- Lobster Poutine
- Maple-Glazed Pork Chops
- Cranberry Sauce
- Butter Chicken Poutine

- Trout Almondine
- Venison Stew
- Maple Walnut Ice Cream
- Corn Chowder
- Montreal-Style Bagels
- Moose Burgers
- Maple Glazed Brussels Sprouts
- Blueberry Muffins
- Campfire Bannock
- Blueberry Sauce
- Roast Beaver Tail Casserole
- Peameal Bacon and Eggs
- Maple Mustard Glazed Chicken
- Wild Mushroom Soup

Poutine

Ingredients:

- French fries (fresh-cut or frozen)
- Cheese curds (white cheddar curds preferred)
- Brown gravy (beef or chicken-based)

Instructions:

1. Cook fries until crispy and hot.
2. Place fries on plate or bowl, scatter cheese curds on top.
3. Pour hot gravy over fries and curds so cheese slightly melts.
4. Serve immediately.

Butter Tarts

Ingredients:

- 1 cup brown sugar
- 1/2 cup corn syrup
- 1/2 cup butter, melted
- 2 eggs
- 1 tsp vanilla extract
- 1 tbsp flour
- Optional: raisins or chopped pecans
- Pastry tart shells

Instructions:

1. Preheat oven to 375°F (190°C).
2. Whisk brown sugar, corn syrup, melted butter, eggs, vanilla, and flour until smooth.
3. Stir in raisins or nuts if using.
4. Pour filling into tart shells about 3/4 full.
5. Bake 15-20 minutes until filling is set but still slightly gooey.
6. Cool before serving.

Nanaimo Bars

Ingredients:

- **Bottom layer:**
    - 1/2 cup butter, melted
    - 1/4 cup sugar
    - 5 tbsp cocoa powder
    - 1 large egg, beaten
    - 1 3/4 cups graham cracker crumbs
    - 1 cup shredded coconut
    - 1/2 cup chopped walnuts
- **Middle layer:**
    - 1/2 cup butter, softened
    - 2 cups powdered sugar
    - 2 tbsp vanilla custard powder or pudding mix
    - 3 tbsp milk
- **Top layer:**
    - 4 oz semi-sweet chocolate
    - 2 tbsp butter

Instructions:

1. Mix melted butter, sugar, cocoa, and egg; stir in crumbs, coconut, walnuts. Press into pan.

2. Beat middle layer ingredients until creamy, spread over base.

3. Melt chocolate and butter, spread over custard layer.

4. Chill until set, then cut into bars.

Tourtière (Meat Pie)

Ingredients:

- 1 lb ground pork (or mix pork and beef)
- 1 small onion, finely chopped
- 1 garlic clove, minced
- 1/2 tsp cinnamon
- 1/4 tsp cloves
- Salt and pepper
- 1/4 cup water or broth
- Pie crust (top and bottom)

Instructions:

1. Cook onion and garlic until translucent. Add meat and brown.
2. Add spices, salt, pepper, and liquid; simmer 10 min.
3. Line pie dish with crust, fill with meat mixture, cover with top crust, seal edges.
4. Bake at 375°F (190°C) for 40-45 minutes until golden.

\Bannock (Traditional Flatbread)

Ingredients:

- 2 cups all-purpose flour
- 1 tbsp baking powder
- 1/2 tsp salt
- 1 tbsp sugar (optional)
- 3/4 cup water or milk
- 2 tbsp melted butter or oil

Instructions:

1. Mix dry ingredients, then add water/milk and butter to form dough.
2. Knead lightly, shape into round flat disc.
3. Cook on griddle or skillet over medium heat, about 5 minutes each side, until golden.
4. Serve warm with butter or jam.

Caesar Cocktail

Ingredients:

- 1 1/2 oz vodka
- 4 oz Clamato juice (tomato and clam juice)
- 2 dashes hot sauce (like Tabasco)
- 2 dashes Worcestershire sauce
- Celery salt and black pepper
- Lime wedge
- Celery stalk or pickle spear for garnish

Instructions:

1. Rim glass with celery salt.
2. Fill glass with ice, add vodka, Clamato, hot sauce, and Worcestershire sauce.
3. Stir gently.
4. Garnish with lime and celery or pickle.

BeaverTails (Fried Dough Pastry)

Ingredients:

- 2 cups all-purpose flour
- 1/2 cup warm water
- 1/2 tsp salt
- 1 tbsp sugar
- 1 tsp yeast
- Oil for frying
- Cinnamon sugar or your favorite toppings

Instructions:

1. Mix yeast, sugar, warm water; let activate 5 minutes.
2. Add flour and salt, knead to dough; let rise until doubled.
3. Roll dough into oval shapes resembling tails.
4. Fry in hot oil until golden.
5. Drain and coat with cinnamon sugar or toppings.

Peameal Bacon Sandwich

Ingredients:

- Peameal bacon (Canadian back bacon), sliced thick
- Soft sandwich bun or Kaiser roll
- Mustard or other preferred condiments
- Lettuce, tomato (optional)

Instructions:

1. Pan-fry peameal bacon slices until browned and cooked.
2. Toast bun lightly.
3. Assemble sandwich with bacon, mustard, and optional veggies.
4. Serve hot.

Maple-Glazed Salmon

Ingredients:

- 4 salmon fillets
- 1/4 cup pure maple syrup
- 2 tbsp soy sauce
- 1 tbsp Dijon mustard
- 1 clove garlic, minced
- Salt and pepper to taste

Instructions:

1. Preheat oven to 400°F (200°C).
2. Mix maple syrup, soy sauce, mustard, and garlic.
3. Place salmon on baking sheet, season with salt and pepper.
4. Brush glaze over salmon.
5. Bake 12-15 minutes, brushing with more glaze halfway through.
6. Serve with steamed veggies or rice.

Split Pea Soup

Ingredients:

- 1 cup dried split peas, rinsed
- 1 onion, diced
- 2 carrots, diced
- 2 celery stalks, diced
- 1 clove garlic, minced
- 6 cups vegetable or chicken broth
- 1 bay leaf
- Salt and pepper to taste
- Optional: diced ham or smoked sausage

Instructions:

1. In a large pot, sauté onion, carrots, celery, and garlic until softened.
2. Add peas, broth, bay leaf, and meat if using.
3. Bring to boil, then simmer for 1-1.5 hours until peas are soft.
4. Remove bay leaf, season with salt and pepper.
5. Blend slightly for creamier texture if desired.

Montreal Smoked Meat Sandwich

Ingredients:

- Montreal smoked meat (or pastrami), sliced
- Rye bread, lightly toasted
- Yellow mustard
- Pickles on the side

Instructions:

1. Pile smoked meat generously on rye bread.
2. Spread mustard on the bread.
3. Serve with pickles.

Maple Syrup Pie

Ingredients:

- 1 1/2 cups pure maple syrup
- 1/4 cup brown sugar
- 3 eggs
- 1/4 cup butter, melted
- 2 tbsp all-purpose flour
- 1 tsp vanilla extract
- 1 unbaked pie crust

Instructions:

1. Preheat oven to 350°F (175°C).
2. In a bowl, whisk eggs, then add syrup, sugar, butter, flour, and vanilla.
3. Pour filling into pie crust.
4. Bake 45-50 minutes until set and golden.
5. Cool before serving.

Lobster Roll

Ingredients:

- 1 lb cooked lobster meat, chopped
- 2 tbsp mayonnaise
- 1 tbsp lemon juice
- 1 tbsp chopped celery
- Salt and pepper to taste
- Buttered and toasted split-top hot dog buns

Instructions:

1. Mix lobster meat with mayonnaise, lemon juice, celery, salt, and pepper.
2. Butter and toast buns.
3. Fill buns with lobster mixture and serve chilled or at room temp.

Chicken and Wild Rice Soup

Ingredients:

- 1 cup cooked wild rice
- 1 lb cooked chicken, shredded
- 1 onion, diced
- 2 carrots, diced
- 2 celery stalks, diced
- 4 cups chicken broth
- 1 cup milk or cream
- 2 tbsp butter
- Salt and pepper to taste

Instructions:

1. Sauté onion, carrots, celery in butter until tender.
2. Add broth, cooked chicken, and wild rice; simmer 10 minutes.
3. Stir in milk or cream, warm gently.
4. Season with salt and pepper.

Saskatoon Berry Pie

Ingredients:

- 4 cups Saskatoon berries (or blueberries/blackberries)
- 3/4 cup sugar
- 1/4 cup flour
- 1 tbsp lemon juice
- 1 unbaked pie crust (top and bottom)

Instructions:

1. Mix berries with sugar, flour, and lemon juice.
2. Pour into pie crust-lined pan, cover with top crust and seal edges.
3. Cut slits in top crust for steam.
4. Bake at 375°F (190°C) for 45-50 minutes until crust is golden.

Maple-Glazed Donuts

Ingredients:

- 2 cups all-purpose flour
- 1/2 cup sugar
- 2 tsp baking powder
- 1/2 tsp salt
- 1/2 cup milk
- 2 eggs
- 1/4 cup butter, melted
- Vegetable oil for frying

Maple Glaze:

- 1 cup powdered sugar
- 2-3 tbsp pure maple syrup
- 1-2 tbsp milk

Instructions:

1. Mix dry ingredients, then wet ingredients separately. Combine to make batter.
2. Heat oil to 350°F (175°C).
3. Drop spoonfuls of batter into oil, fry until golden and cooked through, about 2-3 minutes per side. Drain on paper towels.
4. Whisk glaze ingredients until smooth, dip warm donuts and let set.

Salmon Candy (Candied Salmon)

Ingredients:

- 1 lb salmon fillet, skin on
- 1/2 cup brown sugar
- 2 tbsp soy sauce
- 1 tbsp maple syrup
- 1 tsp smoked paprika (optional)

Instructions:

1. Mix brown sugar, soy sauce, maple syrup, and paprika.
2. Marinate salmon in mixture for at least 1 hour.
3. Preheat oven to 375°F (190°C).
4. Place salmon on baking sheet lined with foil.
5. Bake 15-20 minutes until caramelized and cooked through.
6. Let cool slightly, slice thinly and serve as a snack or appetizer.

Cream of Mushroom Soup

Ingredients:

- 2 cups mushrooms, sliced
- 1 small onion, chopped
- 3 tbsp butter
- 3 tbsp flour
- 4 cups chicken or vegetable broth
- 1 cup cream or milk
- Salt and pepper to taste

Instructions:

1. Sauté onions and mushrooms in butter until soft.
2. Stir in flour and cook 1-2 minutes to form a roux.
3. Slowly whisk in broth, bring to simmer.
4. Add cream, season with salt and pepper.
5. Simmer until thickened, blend partially if desired for creamier texture.

Blueberry Grunt

Ingredients:

- 4 cups fresh or frozen blueberries
- 1/2 cup sugar
- 1 tbsp lemon juice
- 1 cup all-purpose flour
- 1 tsp baking powder
- 1/4 tsp salt
- 1/2 cup milk
- 2 tbsp butter, melted

Instructions:

1. In a saucepan, cook blueberries, sugar, and lemon juice until bubbly.
2. Mix flour, baking powder, salt, milk, and butter into a batter.
3. Drop spoonfuls of batter onto simmering berries.
4. Cover and cook until dumplings are cooked through, about 10-15 minutes.
5. Serve warm, often with cream.

Rappie Pie (Acadian Potato Pie)

Ingredients:

- 4 cups grated raw potatoes
- 2 cups cooked shredded chicken or pork
- 1 onion, chopped
- 1/2 cup chicken broth
- Salt and pepper
- Butter for dotting

Instructions:

1. Squeeze excess moisture from grated potatoes.
2. Layer shredded meat and onion in baking dish.
3. Mix potatoes with broth, season with salt and pepper, and spread over meat.
4. Dot with butter.
5. Bake at 350°F (175°C) for about 1.5 hours until potatoes are golden and cooked.

Fish and Brewis

Ingredients:

- Salted cod, soaked overnight, drained
- Hard bread or hardtack, soaked overnight
- 1 onion, sliced
- 2 tbsp butter
- Pepper to taste

Instructions:

1. Boil soaked cod until tender, flake into pieces.
2. Boil soaked bread until soft and cut into pieces.
3. Mix cod and bread together.
4. Melt butter with sautéed onions, pour over mixture.
5. Serve warm.

Indian Butter Chicken

Ingredients:

- 1 lb chicken breast, cut into pieces
- 1 cup plain yogurt
- 2 tbsp butter
- 1 onion, chopped
- 3 cloves garlic, minced
- 1 tbsp ginger, minced
- 1 can (14 oz) tomato puree
- 1 cup cream
- 2 tsp garam masala
- 1 tsp turmeric
- 1 tsp cumin
- 1 tsp chili powder
- Salt to taste

Instructions:

1. Marinate chicken in yogurt and 1 tsp garam masala for 1 hour.
2. Sauté onion, garlic, and ginger in butter until soft.
3. Add spices (except cream) and cook 1-2 minutes.

4. Add tomato puree and simmer 10 minutes.

5. Add chicken and cook until done.

6. Stir in cream, heat through.

7. Serve with rice or naan.

Ginger Beef

Ingredients:

- 1 lb beef sirloin, thinly sliced
- 1/4 cup soy sauce
- 2 tbsp brown sugar
- 2 tbsp cornstarch
- 1 tbsp grated fresh ginger
- 2 cloves garlic, minced
- 1/4 cup vegetable oil
- 1/2 cup sliced green onions
- 1/2 cup thinly sliced bell peppers (optional)

Instructions:

1. Toss beef with cornstarch.
2. Heat oil, fry beef quickly until crispy, remove.
3. Sauté garlic and ginger, add soy sauce and sugar, bring to simmer.
4. Return beef, toss to coat and heat through.
5. Add green onions and peppers just before serving.

Ketchup Chips

Note: These are a popular Canadian snack sold commercially; homemade version inspired.

Ingredients:

- Thinly sliced potatoes
- 2 tbsp tomato powder or ketchup powder (or mix tomato paste and seasoning)
- 1 tsp vinegar powder or a dash of vinegar
- 1 tsp sugar
- 1/2 tsp salt
- 1/2 tsp onion powder
- Oil for frying

Instructions:

1. Fry potato slices until crisp.
2. Toss hot chips in seasoning mixture.
3. Serve immediately.

Maple-Glazed Carrots

Ingredients:

- 1 lb carrots, peeled and cut
- 2 tbsp butter
- 2 tbsp pure maple syrup
- Salt and pepper

Instructions:

1. Boil or steam carrots until just tender.
2. In a pan, melt butter and add maple syrup.
3. Add carrots, toss to coat, cook a few minutes until glazed.
4. Season with salt and pepper.

Wild Game Stew

Ingredients:

- 2 lbs wild game meat (venison, elk, moose), cubed
- 3 tbsp vegetable oil
- 1 large onion, chopped
- 3 carrots, sliced
- 3 celery stalks, sliced
- 3 potatoes, cubed
- 4 cups beef or game broth
- 2 cups red wine (optional)
- 2 cloves garlic, minced
- 2 bay leaves
- 1 tsp thyme
- Salt and pepper

Instructions:

1. Brown meat in oil over medium-high heat, set aside.
2. Sauté onion, carrots, celery in the same pot until softened.
3. Add garlic, cook 1 minute.
4. Return meat to pot, add broth, wine, bay leaves, thyme, salt, and pepper.

5. Bring to boil, reduce heat, simmer covered 2-3 hours until meat tender.

6. Add potatoes last 30 minutes. Remove bay leaves before serving.

Pea Soup with Ham

Ingredients:

- 1 1/2 cups dried yellow split peas, rinsed
- 1 smoked ham hock or 1 1/2 cups cooked diced ham
- 1 onion, chopped
- 2 carrots, diced
- 2 celery stalks, diced
- 6 cups water or broth
- Salt and pepper

Instructions:

1. In a large pot, combine peas, ham hock, onion, carrots, celery, and water.
2. Bring to boil, reduce to simmer and cook 1.5-2 hours until peas are soft.
3. Remove ham hock, shred meat, return to pot.
4. Season with salt and pepper.

Blueberry Buckle

Ingredients:

- 2 cups all-purpose flour
- 1 1/2 tsp baking powder
- 1/2 tsp salt
- 1/2 cup sugar
- 1/2 cup butter, softened
- 1 large egg
- 1/2 cup milk
- 2 cups fresh blueberries

For the topping:

- 1/4 cup sugar
- 1/2 tsp cinnamon
- 2 tbsp butter, melted

Instructions:

1. Preheat oven to 350°F (175°C).
2. Mix flour, baking powder, salt.
3. Beat sugar and butter until fluffy; add egg.
4. Alternate adding flour and milk to batter.

5. Fold in blueberries.

6. Pour into greased pan.

7. Mix topping ingredients and sprinkle on top.

8. Bake 40-45 minutes until golden and toothpick comes out clean.

Maple Baked Beans

Ingredients:

- 2 cups dried navy or white beans, soaked overnight
- 6 cups water
- 1 onion, chopped
- 1/2 cup pure maple syrup
- 1/4 cup molasses
- 2 tbsp mustard
- 4 slices bacon, chopped (optional)
- Salt and pepper

Instructions:

1. Drain beans, put in pot with water and onion. Simmer 1.5 hours until tender.
2. Drain, then combine beans with maple syrup, molasses, mustard, bacon in baking dish.
3. Add enough water to just cover beans.
4. Bake at 300°F (150°C) for 3-4 hours, adding water if dry.
5. Season to taste.

Clam Chowder

Ingredients:

- 4 cups chopped clams (fresh or canned) with juice
- 3 cups potatoes, diced
- 1 onion, chopped
- 2 celery stalks, chopped
- 4 slices bacon, chopped
- 2 cups milk or cream
- 2 tbsp butter
- 2 tbsp flour
- Salt and pepper

Instructions:

1. Cook bacon in pot until crisp, remove some fat if too much.
2. Sauté onion and celery in bacon fat and butter until soft.
3. Stir in flour, cook 2 minutes.
4. Gradually add clam juice, stirring to thicken.
5. Add potatoes and simmer until tender.
6. Add clams and milk/cream, heat through.
7. Season and serve.

Cabbage Rolls

Ingredients:

- 1 large head cabbage
- 1 lb ground beef or pork
- 1 cup cooked rice
- 1 small onion, diced
- 1 egg
- Salt and pepper
- 2 cups tomato sauce

Instructions:

1. Core cabbage, blanch whole leaves in boiling water until pliable.
2. Mix meat, rice, onion, egg, salt, and pepper.
3. Place meat mix on cabbage leaves, roll up and tuck sides.
4. Place rolls in baking dish, cover with tomato sauce.
5. Bake at 350°F (175°C) for 1-1.5 hours until cooked.

Wild Blueberry Pancakes

Ingredients:

- 1 1/2 cups all-purpose flour
- 3 1/2 tsp baking powder
- 1 tsp salt
- 1 tbsp sugar
- 1 1/4 cups milk
- 1 egg
- 3 tbsp melted butter
- 1 cup wild blueberries

Instructions:

1. Mix flour, baking powder, salt, sugar.
2. Whisk milk, egg, and butter.
3. Combine wet and dry ingredients gently, fold in blueberries.
4. Cook on greased griddle until bubbles form; flip and cook until golden.

Lobster Poutine

Ingredients:

- 4 cups cooked French fries
- 1 cup cheese curds
- 1 1/2 cups lobster meat, cooked and chopped
- 1 1/2 cups lobster or seafood gravy (recipe below)

Lobster Gravy:

- 2 tbsp butter
- 2 tbsp flour
- 1 cup lobster stock or seafood broth
- Salt and pepper

Instructions:

1. Melt butter, whisk in flour to make roux.
2. Slowly add lobster stock, whisk until thickened. Season.
3. Place fries on plate, top with cheese curds, lobster meat, and pour hot gravy over.
4. Serve immediately.

Maple-Glazed Pork Chops

Ingredients:

- 4 pork chops, bone-in or boneless
- Salt and pepper
- 2 tbsp olive oil
- 1/4 cup pure maple syrup
- 2 tbsp Dijon mustard
- 1 tbsp apple cider vinegar
- 1 clove garlic, minced

Instructions:

1. Season pork chops with salt and pepper.
2. Heat olive oil in a skillet over medium-high heat.
3. Sear pork chops 3-4 minutes per side until golden.
4. In a bowl, whisk maple syrup, mustard, vinegar, and garlic.
5. Pour glaze over chops in skillet, reduce heat to medium-low.
6. Cook, turning chops and spooning glaze, until cooked through and glaze thickens (~5 minutes).
7. Serve with extra glaze drizzled on top.

Cranberry Sauce

Ingredients:

- 12 oz fresh cranberries
- 1 cup sugar
- 1 cup water
- Zest and juice of 1 orange
- 1/2 tsp cinnamon (optional)

Instructions:

1. In a saucepan, combine cranberries, sugar, water, orange zest, and juice.
2. Bring to boil, reduce heat and simmer 10 minutes until cranberries pop and sauce thickens.
3. Stir in cinnamon if desired.
4. Cool before serving.

Butter Chicken Poutine

Ingredients:

- 4 cups French fries, hot and crispy
- 1 cup cheese curds
- 2 cups butter chicken sauce (see Butter Chicken recipe from earlier)
- 1 cup cooked chicken, shredded or cubed

Instructions:

1. Arrange fries on a plate or dish.
2. Sprinkle cheese curds over fries.
3. Top with chicken pieces.
4. Ladle hot butter chicken sauce over all to melt cheese.
5. Serve immediately.

Trout Almondine

Ingredients:

- 4 trout fillets
- Salt and pepper
- 3 tbsp butter
- 1/3 cup sliced almonds
- 1 tbsp lemon juice
- 2 tbsp chopped parsley

Instructions:

1. Season trout fillets with salt and pepper.
2. In a skillet, melt 2 tbsp butter over medium heat.
3. Cook trout skin-side down 3-4 minutes per side until cooked through. Remove and keep warm.
4. Add remaining butter to skillet, toast almonds until golden.
5. Stir in lemon juice and parsley.
6. Spoon almond butter sauce over trout and serve.

Venison Stew

Ingredients:

- 2 lbs venison, cubed
- 3 tbsp vegetable oil
- 1 onion, chopped
- 3 carrots, sliced
- 2 celery stalks, sliced
- 3 potatoes, cubed
- 4 cups beef or venison broth
- 2 cups red wine (optional)
- 2 cloves garlic, minced
- 2 bay leaves
- 1 tsp thyme
- Salt and pepper

Instructions:

1. Brown venison in oil, set aside.
2. Sauté onion, carrots, celery until soft.
3. Add garlic, cook 1 minute.
4. Return venison to pot with broth, wine, bay leaves, thyme, salt, and pepper.

5. Simmer covered 2-3 hours until meat is tender.

6. Add potatoes 30 minutes before done. Remove bay leaves before serving.

Maple Walnut Ice Cream

Ingredients:

- 2 cups heavy cream
- 1 cup whole milk
- 3/4 cup pure maple syrup
- 4 egg yolks
- 1 cup chopped toasted walnuts

Instructions:

1. Heat cream, milk, and half the maple syrup until simmering.
2. Whisk egg yolks with remaining maple syrup.
3. Slowly temper yolks with hot cream mixture.
4. Return to heat and cook, stirring, until custard thickens.
5. Cool, then churn in ice cream maker according to manufacturer instructions.
6. Fold in walnuts during last few minutes of churning. Freeze until firm.

Corn Chowder

Ingredients:

- 4 cups corn kernels (fresh or frozen)
- 2 slices bacon, chopped
- 1 onion, chopped
- 2 potatoes, diced
- 3 cups chicken or vegetable broth
- 1 cup cream or milk
- Salt and pepper
- 2 tbsp butter

Instructions:

1. Cook bacon in pot until crisp, remove some fat if desired.
2. Sauté onion and butter in bacon fat until soft.
3. Add potatoes and broth, simmer until potatoes are tender.
4. Add corn, cook 5-7 minutes.
5. Stir in cream, season, and heat through.

Montreal-Style Bagels

Ingredients:

- 4 cups bread flour
- 1 tbsp sugar
- 1 tbsp honey
- 1 1/4 tsp salt
- 2 tsp instant yeast
- 1 1/4 cups warm water
- 1 tbsp vegetable oil
- 2 tbsp honey (for boiling)
- Sesame seeds or poppy seeds for topping

Instructions:

1. Mix flour, sugar, salt, yeast.
2. Add warm water and oil, knead to smooth dough.
3. Let rise 1 hour.
4. Divide into 10 balls, shape into bagels.
5. Let rest 20 minutes.
6. Boil water with honey; boil bagels 1 minute each side.
7. Drain, place on baking sheet, sprinkle with seeds.

8. Bake at 425°F (220°C) for 20-25 minutes until golden.

Moose Burgers

Ingredients:

- 1 lb ground moose (or lean ground venison)
- 1 small onion, finely chopped
- 2 cloves garlic, minced
- 1 egg
- 1/4 cup breadcrumbs (optional)
- 1 tbsp Worcestershire sauce
- Salt and pepper to taste
- Burger buns and toppings (lettuce, tomato, cheese, etc.)

Instructions:

1. In a bowl, combine moose meat, onion, garlic, egg, breadcrumbs, Worcestershire sauce, salt, and pepper.
2. Form into 4 patties.
3. Grill or pan-fry over medium heat for 4-5 minutes per side, or until cooked through.
4. Serve on buns with your favorite toppings.

Maple Glazed Brussels Sprouts

Ingredients:

- 1 lb Brussels sprouts, halved
- 2 tbsp olive oil
- Salt and pepper
- 3 tbsp pure maple syrup
- 1 tbsp balsamic vinegar (optional)

Instructions:

1. Toss Brussels sprouts with olive oil, salt, and pepper.
2. Roast at 400°F (200°C) for 20-25 minutes until tender and caramelized.
3. Drizzle with maple syrup and balsamic vinegar, toss gently, roast another 5 minutes.
4. Serve warm.

Blueberry Muffins

Ingredients:

- 2 cups all-purpose flour
- 3/4 cup sugar
- 2 tsp baking powder
- 1/2 tsp salt
- 1/2 cup vegetable oil
- 1 cup milk
- 2 large eggs
- 1 1/2 cups fresh or frozen blueberries

Instructions:

1. Preheat oven to 375°F (190°C). Grease or line muffin tin.
2. Mix flour, sugar, baking powder, and salt in a bowl.
3. In another bowl, whisk oil, milk, and eggs.
4. Combine wet and dry ingredients just until mixed. Fold in blueberries.
5. Fill muffin cups 2/3 full.
6. Bake 20-25 minutes until a toothpick comes out clean.

Campfire Bannock

Ingredients:

- 2 cups all-purpose flour
- 2 tsp baking powder
- 1/2 tsp salt
- 1 tbsp sugar
- 1/2 cup water (more if needed)
- 1/4 cup vegetable oil or melted butter

Instructions:

1. Mix dry ingredients in a bowl.
2. Add water and oil; stir to form a dough.
3. Knead lightly on floured surface, shape into a flat round.
4. Cook over campfire coals or in a skillet on medium heat, about 5-7 minutes each side until golden and cooked through.
5. Serve with jam, honey, or savory toppings.

Blueberry Sauce

Ingredients:

- 2 cups blueberries (fresh or frozen)
- 1/4 cup sugar
- 1/4 cup water
- 1 tbsp lemon juice
- 1 tsp cornstarch mixed with 1 tbsp water (optional, for thickening)

Instructions:

1. In a saucepan, combine blueberries, sugar, water, and lemon juice.
2. Simmer over medium heat 10 minutes until blueberries burst and sauce thickens.
3. If desired, stir in cornstarch slurry and cook another 1-2 minutes to thicken.
4. Cool slightly and serve warm or cold over pancakes, muffins, or desserts.

Roast Beaver Tail Casserole

(Note: "Beaver tail" here refers to the traditional meat, but if unavailable, substitute with beef or pork.)

Ingredients:

- 2 lbs beaver tail meat or beef/pork stew meat, cubed
- 2 tbsp vegetable oil
- 1 onion, chopped
- 3 cloves garlic, minced
- 3 carrots, sliced
- 3 potatoes, diced
- 2 cups beef broth
- 1 cup mushrooms, sliced
- 1 cup peas (fresh or frozen)
- 2 tbsp tomato paste
- 1 tsp thyme
- Salt and pepper to taste
- 1/4 cup flour (optional, for thickening)

Instructions:

1. Preheat oven to 350°F (175°C).
2. In a large skillet, heat oil and brown the meat on all sides. Remove and set aside.

3. In the same skillet, sauté onion and garlic until translucent.

4. Add carrots, potatoes, mushrooms, and tomato paste; cook 5 minutes.

5. Return meat to skillet, sprinkle flour over, stir well.

6. Add broth and thyme, season with salt and pepper. Bring to simmer.

7. Transfer everything to a casserole dish, cover with foil, and bake for 1.5 to 2 hours until meat is tender.

8. Stir in peas during the last 10 minutes of baking.

Peameal Bacon and Eggs

Ingredients:

- 8 slices peameal bacon (Canadian back bacon)
- 4 large eggs
- Butter or oil for cooking
- Salt and pepper to taste

Instructions:

1. Heat a skillet over medium heat and cook peameal bacon slices until golden and cooked through (~3 minutes per side). Remove and keep warm.
2. In the same skillet, add butter or oil and cook eggs sunny side up or to your preference. Season with salt and pepper.
3. Serve eggs atop or alongside peameal bacon slices.

Maple Mustard Glazed Chicken

Ingredients:

- 4 chicken thighs (bone-in, skin-on recommended)
- Salt and pepper
- 2 tbsp olive oil
- 1/4 cup pure maple syrup
- 2 tbsp Dijon mustard
- 1 tbsp apple cider vinegar
- 1 clove garlic, minced

Instructions:

1. Preheat oven to 400°F (200°C).
2. Season chicken with salt and pepper. Heat olive oil in an ovenproof skillet over medium-high heat.
3. Sear chicken, skin side down, until golden (about 5 minutes). Flip and cook 2 minutes.
4. Mix maple syrup, mustard, vinegar, and garlic in a bowl.
5. Brush glaze over chicken. Transfer skillet to oven and roast 20-25 minutes until cooked through.
6. Baste with glaze once or twice during roasting.

Wild Mushroom Soup

Ingredients:

- 1 lb mixed wild mushrooms, cleaned and sliced
- 2 tbsp butter
- 1 onion, chopped
- 2 cloves garlic, minced
- 4 cups vegetable or chicken broth
- 1/2 cup heavy cream
- 1 tbsp fresh thyme leaves
- Salt and pepper to taste
- Fresh parsley for garnish

Instructions:

1. Melt butter in a large pot over medium heat. Add onion and garlic, cook until soft.
2. Add mushrooms and thyme, cook until mushrooms release their juices and start to brown (~10 minutes).
3. Pour in broth, bring to a boil, then simmer 15 minutes.
4. Use an immersion blender to puree some or all of the soup for desired texture (optional).
5. Stir in cream, season with salt and pepper, heat through but do not boil.
6. Garnish with parsley and serve.

www.ingramcontent.com/pod-product-compliance
Lightning Source LLC
LaVergne TN
LVHW081319060526
838201LV00055B/2364